First published in 2005 by Myriad
Books Limited
35 Bishopsthorpe Road,
London SE26 4PA

Photographs copyright
© John Potter
Text copyright © John Potter

John Potter has asserted his right
under the Copyright, Designs and
Patents Act 1998 to be identified as
the author of this work.

*The author and publisher are
grateful to Lord Clifford of Chudleigh
for permission to photograph in the
grounds of Skipton Castle.*

ISBN 1 904 736 11 4

Designed by Jerry Goldie Graphic
Design
Map artwork by Stephen Dew

Printed in China

www.myriadbooks.com

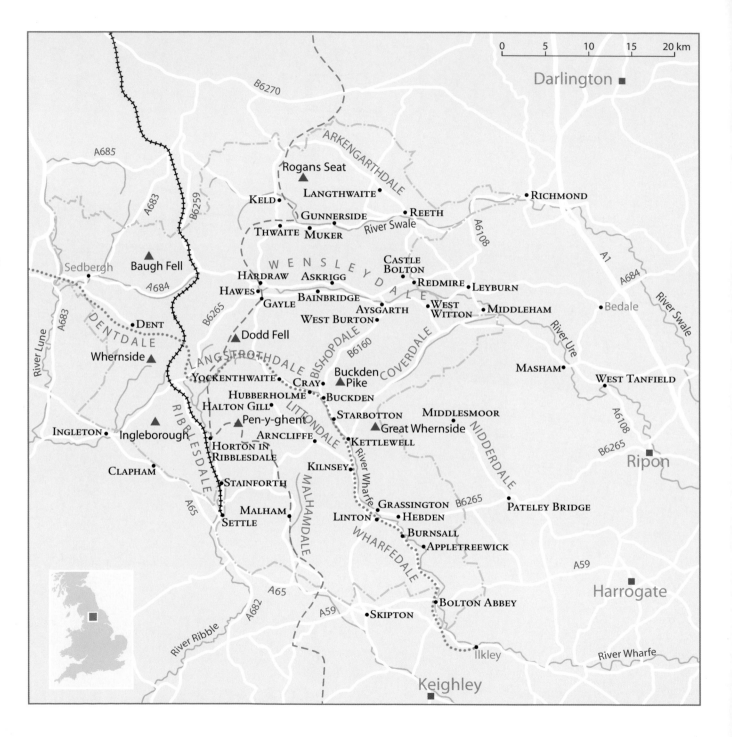

Key

- – – – The Pennine Way
- ········· The Dales Way
- ┼┼┼┼┼ The Settle to Carlisle Railway
- ▲ Peaks
- –·–·– Yorkshire Dales National Park boundary

Contents

APPLETREEWICK

Four miles south-east of Grassington, this peaceful Wharfedale village rests on a steep slope overlooked by the craggy summit of Simon's Seat. The main street is lined by ornate and characterful cottages and at either end there is Low Hall and High Hall

Sir William Craven, Appletreewick's most famous inhabitant, was known as "Dick Whittington of the Dales". A farmer's son, he was sent to London to make his fortune. He became Lord Mayor in 1610! Sir William rebuilt High Hall and the building is still to be found at the top of the hill.

The local community in Appletreewick pride themselves on the fact that almost all of the properties are

occupied by residents living in the village. They enjoy the benefit of having two public houses, cricket, darts and domino teams as well as the small but beautiful church, St John's (opposite, left).

As can be seen (left), Appletreewick nestles snugly on a south-facing slope above the river Wharfe and is surrounded by some of the most beautiful scenery in Wharfedale; to the right is the summit of Simon's Seat. This photograph was taken from the slopes of Burnsall Fell.

The very distinctive Mock Beggar Hall (below) in the centre of the village was built on the site of a grange used by the monks of Bolton Priory. It is rumoured that one particularly wayward monk was walled up inside the hall.

ARNCLIFFE

Arncliffe lies at the heart of Littondale, one of the loveliest of the Dales. It is the largest of the four settlements in the dale, which include the village of Litton and the small hamlets of Halton Gill and remote Foxup. Just six miles north-west of Grassington, Arncliffe sits comfortably by the river Skirfare on a well-drained gravel delta above the flood plain

Arncliffe has a central wide open green, surrounded by mellow stone cottages and farm buildings. Several large porched barns point to the fact that this is a typical Dales' working community. The days of muckspreading by hand from horse and cart, and taking hay to the fields on horseback, are distant memories now and a far more familiar sound is that of the quad bike.

Littondale was the setting for part of Charles Kingsley's novel *The Water Babies*, and it was also chosen originally as the setting for the long-running and very popular ITV series *Emmerdale*. A much-loved characteristic of the village is the large number of hardwood trees that surround the church and stretch along the river bank.

The Church of St Oswald's lies close to the stone bridge over the river Skirfare. Nearly all of the stained-glass windows are Victorian. In the sidelights of the east window are depicted St Michael and St Oswald, the patron saints of Hubberholme and Arncliffe respectively.

Artists and photographers in search of inspiration need only stroll down one of several quiet lanes leading from the village green. The hinge, horseshoe and feather were found on a nearby chicken hut. Perhaps they were arranged to encourage the laying of more eggs!

ASKRIGG

Just two miles north-west of Bainbridge in Wensleydale, Askrigg sits comfortably below the slopes of Askrigg Common on a quiet minor road that links Leyburn to Hardraw

Askrigg is perhaps best known as the setting for the popular television series *All Creatures Great and Small*. The country vet James Herriot's home Skeldale House in the series is actually Cringly House which can be found in the old marketplace. Saint Oswald's in the centre of the village is a beautiful 15th-century church with a tall tower, a broad nave and a fine nave roof.

The skyline across the valley from Askrigg is dominated by the unmistakeable form of Addlebrough and the colours and textures on its lower slopes are beautifully highlighted as the sun sets at the western end of the dale. Visitors to the village should take care when sitting on this bench (above) and certainly not leave their packed-lunch unattended!

An annual carnival with parades, music and children's races brings the community together each year in the centre of the village. The young children of the village are seen, left, setting off to race round the village. Who knows, in years to come, perhaps one will become a fell race champion!

AYSGARTH

The village of Aysgarth is situated seven miles west of Leyburn on the A684 and is probably best known for its spectacular waterfalls that cascade down a series of large limestone steps, making it one of Wensleydale's most popular attractions

A series of delightful riverside walks link the Upper, Middle and Lower Aysgarth Falls. Known collectively as Aysgarth Force, the three sets of falls are all within one mile of each other. The best view of the Upper Force is from the 16th-century bridge, which spans the river Ure. There is a national park information centre and a large car park within easy strolling distance of the falls. In early spring the riverside woodland walks are adorned with a beautiful white carpet of wood anenomes.

Aysgarth is in the Deanery of Wensley in the Archdeaconry of Richmond, which is now in the Diocese of Ripon. In earliest times Wensleydale was divided into two main ancient parishes, Aysgarth

Wood anenome *Anenome nemerosa*

and Wensley. St Andrew's Church, just a few minutes stroll from the falls has, reputedly, the largest churchyard in Britain, which is over four acres in size, together with many outstanding features. The rood screen (right) was carved by the Ripon School of Carvers in 1506 and is said to have been taken from Jervaulx Abbey after the dissolution of the monasteries in the reign of Henry VIII.

BAINBRIDGE

The village of Bainbridge, set in the heart of Wensleydale on the A684, has a wide and sweeping village green with ancient village stocks and mature hardwood trees, overlooked from the east by the remains of an unexcavated Roman settlement

In Norman times the great forest of Wensleydale dominated the area and forest workers lived in the village. Each evening the Bainbridge hornblower would sound his horn to guide them, and travellers, back to the village. The custom continues to this day – every year from the 27th of September during the Feast of the Holy Rood the horn is still sounded at 10pm. It is kept hanging in the Rose and Crown Inn on the village green.

The surrounding area of Upper Wensleydale is well known for its hay meadows, pastures and stone buildings. Artefacts found in earthworks from the Bronze and Iron Age, now kept in the Dales Countryside Museum in Hawes, tell us that Anglian and Norse settlers were farming in these parts many years ago.

13

BOLTON ABBEY

Bolton Bridge, on the A59 just five miles west of Skipton, is the gateway to Wharfedale. It is but a stone's throw from Bolton Abbey, a beautiful Augustinian priory

Bolton Abbey is immensely popular with visitors, many of whom stay close to the monastic buildings, often choosing to picnic and spend the whole day by the river. Those who venture a little further along the splendid riverside walks will find some of Wharfedale's most popular attractions.

Two of the most spectacular are "the Strid" – the narrow chasm through which the river Wharfe gushes in a thunderous cascade – and the enchanting Valley of Desolation with its waterfalls and wooded glades. Further upstream, along a nature trail, can be found Barden Bridge and the beautifully sited Barden Tower, which was built in 1485 by Lord Henry Clifford, and restored by Lady Anne Clifford in 1658-59. The photographs here of hoar frosts and spring bluebells illustrate this immensely popular and idyllic location through the seasons.

BUCKDEN

The village of Buckden, four miles north of Kettlewell on the B6160, is very popular among walkers; paths lead from the village in all directions, making it the perfect base for exploring Wharfedale with its glorious scenery

The annual Buckden Pike Fell Race is a great draw for runners from across the north of England, and it's an exciting spectacle to see such fit athletes powering their way up steep inclines as they aim for the summit of Buckden Pike. The race is 4 miles (6.4km) long and finishes on the gala field after a climb of 1,500ft (450m) to the top and back.

Lower down on the village green at the gala (far right) it's a serious time when the judge has to decide who has the best Swaledale ewes.

To amble through Wharfedale's glorious wildflower meadows in spring is truly a wonderful and most memorable experience. This was a particularly good year for bistort (*Polygonum bistorta*) the tall perennial herb. Starting from the village, a much-loved triangular walk of approximately seven miles takes in the small hamlets of Cray, Yockenthwaite and Hubberholme. Part of the walk includes a short

section of Roman road along Buckden Rake which provides superb views west across the head of Wharfedale into Langstrothdale from a gallery footpath on a natural limestone shelf.

Close to the summit of Buckden Pike is a well-known memorial to the Polish crew of an aircraft that crashed here in 1942. There was just one survivor who managed to reach safety by following the tracks of a fox in the snow.

BURNSALL

Burnsall, 10 miles north-west of Ilkley, is famous for its massive five-arched bridge, which spans the river Wharfe. It is one of the most photographed of all the Dales' villages

Every August the village of Burnsall hosts England's oldest fell race. This event is hugely popular, both for locals and visitors alike. There is a wonderful carnival atmosphere to be experienced throughout the day, usually with a brass band playing. There are family races, and many other traditional community country sports taking place on the village green.

Burnsall is everything a Dales' village should be. Its shape is very much dictated by the river Wharfe. Many of the houses date back to the 17th century and are built from rich warm stone. The photograph of the village in the winter (left) was taken from Rowan Tree Crag shortly after sunrise in February.

A trip to the Dales would not be complete without visiting one of the many outstanding churches, and Wharfedale has its fair share of them. The parish church of St Wilfred is a fine example and can be approached via a unique lych-gate. The church was founded in the 12th century by de Romilles of Skipton. This 19th-century stained-glass panel is a memorial to William Stockdale (1747-1836) and his wife Sarah (1768-1848).

CASTLE BOLTON

The small village of Castle Bolton, five miles west of Leyburn, is dominated by Bolton Castle. There is a wide green in the centre of the village and a very attractive 14th-century church, St Oswald's, which nestles in the shadow of the impressive Bolton Castle

The massive fortress of Bolton Castle (right) has dominated Wensleydale since 1379 and can be seen for miles around. It is one of the

This unusual wrought-iron gate arch is sited close to the small and ancient St Oswald's church

country's best preserved castles; Mary Queen of Scots was imprisoned here during 1568 and 1569. The photograph (above) looking south across Wensleydale was taken from its delightful herb garden. Two of the castle gardens, the Herb Garden and the Walled Garden, have been restored along medieval lines, and should not be missed, providing visitors with a beautiful setting and wonderful views of the dale. The photograph (far left) was taken from St Oswald's looking towards the old post office and village green. The village of Grinton in Swaledale, with its interesting church and picturesque Bridge Inn, can be reached from a minor moor road at the eastern end of the village.

CLAPHAM

Clapham is a blissful haven for visitors just off the busy A65 six miles north-west of Settle. It is a focal point for walks to Selside, Austwick and Horton-in-Ribblesdale. It is also a perfect base for exploring the remote and beautiful Crummackdale where the famous Norber erratic boulders are located

The beautiful Clapham Beck, left, flows through the centre of the village, and passes beneath four bridges. The village is very much more wooded than most other Dales' villages, thanks mainly to the Farrer family who, in the early 18th century, developed Clapham as an estate village. Ingleborough Hall was rebuilt, and Clapham Beck was planted with thousands of trees including larch, pine, spruce and many hardwoods. The Ingleborough Trail leads through these mature woodlands to Ingleborough Cave and Gaping Gill, a cavern the size of York Minster.

The beck was dammed to create a lake which changed the character of the top part of the village. Close by stands the Church of St James which was founded in Norman times. The angel window display in the porch, together with many more displays in the church, were part of the Myths and Legends Festival in the year 2004. The festival celebrated the 50th anniversary of the Yorkshire Dales becoming a national park. In 1954 the Yorkshire Dales became a national park because of the wide range of wildlife, the varied habitats, and the unique and beautiful scenery, together with traditional trades, crafts and local history. Over 20,000 residents live and work in the national park and the area covers 1,773 square kilometres.

CRAY

The little hamlet of Cray nestles at the southern end of Bishopdale one and a half miles north of Buckden. It is the starting point for many walks and its famous inn, The White Lion, is the highest pub in Wharfedale

Cray consists of a scatter of stone houses and farm buildings and is situated about halfway up Buckden Pike, below Kidstones Pass. It is very accessible from Skipton, lying as it does on the B6160 between Wharfedale and Wensleydale. It is a useful starting point for ramblers and could provide an overnight stop for those walking the Dales Way.

The barn in the photograph (above) is typical of those in the southern dales, many of which were built between 1750 and 1850. Barn walls are very similar in construction to the drystone walls of the fields – two faced edges are constructed together with a packing of smaller stones and bonding stones, or "throughs" (large pieces of quarried stone) are used to hold together the outer and inner skins of barn walls.

Cray Gill runs into the river Wharfe a couple of miles south of the village and is fed by several smaller gills which cascade over rocky outcrops forming beautiful waterfalls. All are within easy walking distance of the village along well-marked footpaths.

DENT

This pretty village is actually in Cumbria four miles south-east of Sedbergh, although it lies within the Yorkshire Dales National Park. It boasts the highest mainline railway station in Britain and is close to two spectacular viaducts on the Settle-Carlisle railway line

Strolling through the narrow cobbled streets of Dent is like travelling back in time. The white-painted cottages (left) are most unusual and very Cumbrian in character. Dent is famous from the poem by Robert Southey which tells of the *Terrible Knitters o' Dent* – so-called because of the knitters' prodigious output of knitwear. At one time everyone in the village knitted in order to supplement their meagre incomes, and the stockings and nightcaps produced were sold locally in markets or taken further afield.

Just four miles from the quiet and peaceful village of Dent, the railway station is the highest on an English main line. This view (right) across the western side of the village shows clearly the campsite (which has excellent facilities) and, beyond, High Hall on the lower slopes of Aye Gill Pike.

In the centre of the village can be found a huge slab of Shap granite (right). This is a memorial to Adam Sedgwick, a native of Dent who went on to become a professor of geology at Cambridge. Cool spring water flows out into a small trough at the base of the monument and provides a welcome drink after walking on the fells or exploring the cobbled streets.

GAYLE

Situated just half a mile north of the lively market town of Hawes, Gayle is a very quiet and picturesque village. At the foot of Sledale, Duerley Beck cascades over a series of limestone steps in the centre of the village before rushing below a packhorse bridge

The broad, sweeping and spectacular landscape of Wensleydale is arguably the most beautiful of all the Yorkshire Dales. Much of the upper dale can be seen from the packhorse bridge where locals often stop to exchange the news of the day and visitors pause to admire the attractive stepped waterfalls of Duerley Beck. Early spring showers often swell the beck causing a torrent of

foaming water to race past the rows of terraced cottages sited on the bank. There is an old cotton mill by the beck, and a stone-flagged causeway leads gently down across meadows to Hawes church. Gayle Mill, situated just downstream from the main bridge, was the winner of the northern heat of the BBC's *Restoration* series (2004). The mill dates from 1776 and has almost all of its working machinery in place. Distinctive patterns of drystone walls and isolated field barns are very characteristic of the Yorkshire Dales. In the past they were an important asset to the farmer, providing enclosed grazing land and a place to house both cattle and the hay to feed them in the winter.

GRASSINGTON

Grassington is the largest settlement in upper Wharfedale and has developed mainly due to its close proximity to the place where two historically important roads cross in the dale. The B6160 from Ilkley to Buckden and beyond meets the B6265 Skipton to Pateley Bridge at Threshfield, just east of this popular village

Grassington has many charming features including a cobbled square complete with an ornate water pump, restored in the year 2000 to commemorate the men in the village who lost their lives in the great wars of the last century. Grassington was granted a charter for a market and fair in 1281, which continued to be held until about 1860. Today's farmers' market is a thriving concern and very popular with both locals and visitors alike. At Christmas the shopkeepers in the village dress in Dickensian costume and transform Grassington into a Victorian village. After dark braziers are set up around the village square and a very authentic atmosphere is recreated.

Grassington is very well placed at the southern tip of the Yorkshire Dales and is one of the most popular towns in the whole of the national park. It is an ideal centre for those who wish to pursue activities such as cycling, camping, riding, walking and exploring the surrounding Dales countryside.

GUNNERSIDE

The village of Gunnerside sits at the foot of Gunnerside Gill, and is an unspoilt, picturesque and very quiet settlement situated just three and a half miles east of Thwaite on the B6270 that links Kirby Stephen with Richmond

The name "Gunnerside" derives from the Norse for "Gunners Pasture", Gunner being a hero in Norse saga. It was very conveniently sited for the men who used to work in the many leadmines in the area. Students of industrial archaeology will find no better place to explore than Gunnerside Gill and the desolate and scarred fells above the village. The drystone walls, out barns and field system patterns in the valley bottom at Gunnerside are unique and most attractive, providing photographers and artists with an abundance of artistic opportunity.

Swaledale is famous the world over for its hardy breed of sheep and glorious wildflower meadows which are a blaze of colour in June and July. Gunnerside Gill (right) leads to the remains of Sir Francis Mine and Melbecks Moor.

HALTON GILL

Situated at the northern end of Littondale and eight miles north-east of Settle, Halton Gill has a most beautiful and quite spectacular setting

Surrounded and sheltered by Plover Hill, Cow Close Fell and Horse Head Moor, the village of Halton Gill sits comfortably beside the infant river Skirfare, which is fed by Cosh Beck, Foxup Beck and Hesleden Beck. The stone houses and farm buildings are mostly 17th century and one barn has a huge entrance porch dated 1829.

A local star in the Dale is pictured below. The black-faced sheep pictured here with Heather Nolan of Wrathmire Farm is Flodden Black Knight, a prizewinning Suffolk tup. He won Supreme Champion at the Suffolk Sale, Skipton in 2003, came first at the Kilnsey Show and was placed second at the Masham Sheep Fair in 2004. The prizewinning ram is jointly owned by Ian, Dawn and son Richard Nolan at Halton Gill, Richard Close of Calf Halls Farm in Starbotton, and John Huck of Church Farm, Hubberholme.

— • —

From top to bottom: motor-cyclists take part in the Allan Jefferies Trophy Trial, an annual event in Halton Gill; a flock of Swaledale sheep being moved through the village; fell runners crossing the packhorse bridge on Gala Day

HARDRAW

The village of Hardraw lies one mile north of Hawes on a very quiet by-road, almost at the foot of Buttertubs Pass – a spectacular link road over the fells from Wensleydale to Thwaite in Swaledale

Hardraw is a stopping off point for walkers on the Pennine Way or those embarking on the ascent of nearby Great Shunner Fell, a bleak and remote summit which, at 2,340ft (713m), offers – in good weather – spectacular views of The Three Peaks, Wensleydale and Swaledale.

The jewel in the crown at Hardraw is very definitely the 96ft (29m) waterfall, Hardraw Force, said to be the highest in England. Walking to the falls along the banks of Fossdale Gill can be slippery, especially in winter or after rainfall. It is possible to walk behind the shimmering cascade but usually only the most intrepid of visitors will attempt this. Hardraw Force is fed by both Fossdale Gill and Hearne Beck. The falls can only be reached by paying a small access fee and going through the Green Dragon Inn in the centre of the village – but the view is well worth the price!

HAWES

*The busy market town of Hawes sits
comfortably between high fells at the head
of Wensleydale, on the trans-Pennine A684
that links Northallerton in North Yorkshire
to Kendal in Cumbria*

Hawes was granted a market charter by William
III in 1699. The name Hawes is derived from the
word *hause* which means a narrow neck of land.
Known as the "little capital" of Upper
Wensleydale it is Yorkshire's highest market
town and has a thriving farming community.
The Hawes Livestock Auction Mart has weekly
sales and is always well attended by both locals
and visitors. The mart serves a large area of the
Yorkshire Dales and the surrounding moorland

and fells. The livestock from the area is famed far and wide for its quality.

Other enterprising local industries include the unusual Hawes Ropeworks and the Wensleydale Creamery where the famous Wensleydale cheese is produced. The town also has a large pottery, a Dales Countryside Museum and, just six miles away at Garsdale station, the Settle-Carlisle Railway line which links the Eden Valley and Ribblesdale with the Three Peaks.

HEBDEN

The small village of Hebden lies on the road to Pateley Bridge and Nidderdale about two miles east of Grassington. Located in an upland valley it is surrounded by rocky crags and picturesque waterfalls

Hebden sits proudly above its beck within a narrow gorge, which is unusual for this area in exposing dark gritstone rock rather than the more familiar limestone.

Hebden brook runs through the village as it makes its way down to the river Wharfe. A quaint packhorse bridge (left) leads over the brook to an idyllic cluster of stone cottages. Beyond these cottages several paths lead up onto Hebden Moor where there are many disused mines and shafts.

The Village Store and Post Office (below) provides a much needed service to the local community, and in high summer a very welcome Yorkshire Dales Old Fashioned Dairy Ice Cream!

HORTON IN RIBBLESDALE

Horton is one of the most popular potholing centres of this region and is an ideal centre from which to explore the caves of upper Ribblesdale. The village is situated six miles north of Settle on the B6479

Horton is known the world over as the starting and finishing point of the famous Three Peaks Walk which includes nearby Pen-y-ghent (right), Ingleborough and Whernside.

The village is one of the most popular stopping places for walkers tackling the Pennine Way. The café provides much more than large pots of refreshing Yorkshire tea; it's also a spot where Three Peaks' walkers clock in and out to register their progress on the well-known trek. Pen-y-ghent, one of the Three Peaks on this walk, is pictured (far right) photographed in midwinter from the Pennine Way near Churn Milk Hole.

The famous Settle to Carlisle railway line passes through Horton and passengers are treated to some of the most spectacular scenery in England. Pen-y-ghent is about three miles from the village and is reached by the Pennine Way footpath, along Scar Lane. Walkers must proceed with caution as the area is dotted with potholes, the biggest being those at Hull and Hunt Pot.

Each year at the Horton Gala there is a tremendous entry of runners in the famous Three Peaks Fell race. They train them young in these parts, as can be seen in the photograph (centre)!

HUBBERHOLME

This tiny village is located on the Dales Way four and a half miles from Kettlewell and is famous for its beautiful church and atmospheric pub

The small hamlet of Hubberholme is set at the foot of Langstrothdale, and consists of a cluster of old farm cottages surrounding the church and the George Inn, pictured here beyond the bridge. St Michael's Church was once flooded so badly that fish were seen swimming in the nave!

Hubberholme was the favourite village of the writer J B Priestley. It is named after a Viking chieftain and is famed for its church of St Michael and All Angels. Literary pilgrims visit the village to see the George Inn where the novelist could often be found enjoying the local ale. The churchyard is the last resting place for his ashes. The roof loft dates from 1558 and is one of very few of this type left in England. The choir stalls and the pews are much more recent and were made in 1934 by Robert Thompson, the

"Mouseman" of Kilburn. This small stained-glass panel is part of a larger window featuring three Archangels, by the artist Francis Skeat, dated 1970.

The George Inn was once a vicarage, and its outside lavatories have these quaint signs (right) to guide users so that Y'ewes and Tups do not get confused. Probably a very useful feature after some of the local ale has been consumed!

Each year Spring Bank Holiday weekend heralds the welcome return of Morris dancers, who fill the air with lively music, laughter and the unmistakeable sound of clogs on stone outside many of the delightful Dales' village pubs.

INGLETON

The pretty market town of Ingleton is set amidst the unique and spectacular landscape of the limestone uplands of the Dales. Situated just six miles south-east of Kirby Lonsdale, it is by-passed by the A65 which follows the route of the historic Keighley-Kendal turnpike

Ingleton nestles in the lee of Ingleborough, one of the famous Three Peaks of the Yorkshire Dales, the others being Pen-y-ghent and Whernside.

The settlement is surrounded by dramatic scenery both below and above ground. The Ingleton waterfalls provide visitors with an amazing series of cascades tumbling down through wooded gorges, and White Scar Cave which brims with thousands of stalactites.

The narrow winding streets of the village centre are clustered around a tiny marketplace. Nearby, the late Victorian church of St Mary's (pictured here on the right) has one of the finest Norman fonts in Yorkshire. There are many hotels, guesthouses and a youth hostel, and golfers will find that there are fantastic views of the area from Ingleton golf course.

St Mary's can be seen here overlooking Bell Horse Gate cottages. Wool and cotton-spinning were very important local industries in the 18th and 19th centuries, and many more terraced workers' cottages are to be found in the shadow of the magnificent Ingleton Viaduct at the bottom of this steep hill. This photograph was taken from the Millennium 2000 garden which is landscaped into the hillside.

KELD

Keld, just off the B6270, is situated in a very remote and attractive setting at the head of Swaledale nine miles south-east of Kirby Stephen. Its name is the old Norse word for a spring

The stone houses of Keld cluster around a chapel, and the village boasts its own literary institute. This photograph (left) was taken from Swallow Hole just north of the village.

The River Swale is fed by many small becks and gills, and just 10 minutes stroll from the village runs East Gill Force (right). This waterfall is not named as such on the OS map but is easily found just north of the Pennine Way where the long-distance footpath crosses East Stonesdale.

Stiles in the northern dales are mostly "squeeze" stiles constructed from large slabs of sandstone which can be easily quarried and split locally.

KETTLEWELL

In the shadow of Great Whernside 13 miles north of Skipton, Kettlewell is popular with potholers, climbers and walkers. Its buildings are clustered close to Cam Beck, near where it joins the river Wharfe

The Scarecrow Festival in Kettlewell (above) has become an increasingly popular community event, attracting ever more visitors to this delightful village each year. Kettlewell's beautiful setting is an ideal place from which to explore the surrounding fells and the river valley.

Many of the stone houses in the village, such as the one on the left with its magnificent garden, date from the 17th and 18th centuries. Kettlewell's popularity with visitors is very well served by numerous holiday cottages and guesthouses.

Low winter sunshine reveals the distinctive pattern of drystone walls and out barns, so typical of the area. These fields (above) lie just south of the village and were photographed from a footpath just above Crookacre Wood. The long-distance footpath, the Dales Way, which links Ilkley to Windermere, runs along the valley bottom at this point.

KILNSEY

The tiny village of Kilnsey lies just three miles north of Grassington on the B6160 in the heart of Wharfedale. It nestles in the shadow of Kilnsey Crag, a dramatic peak much loved by climbers

Together with its glorious setting, Kilnsey has many attractions. These include the long-distance footpath, the Dales Way, which passes close by and pony-trekking from the village of Conistone just half a mile away across the valley. There is also fly-fishing and a nature trail at Kilnsey Park Trout Farm. The very popular Tennants Arms provides a warm and friendly welcome, so typical of Dales' pubs.

Kilnsey Crag towers high over the village – 170ft (52m) above the nearby B6160 – and is the most prominent landmark in Wharfedale. The 40ft (12m) overhang at the top provides an irresistible challenge to climbers and passing walkers are often to be seen gazing up in astonishment at their daring and agility.

The Kilnsey Agricultural Show is a showcase for the local farming community. Held every year on the Tuesday after the August Bank Holiday against the backdrop of Kilnsey Crag, it is the ideal opportunity for the older characters of the dale to get together and catch up on local news and events.

Ian Nolan together with his daughter Heather from Halton Gill, and their prizewinning restored tractor and trailer

LANGTHWAITE

Arkengarthdale is Yorkshire's most northern dale and is noted for its scenic attractions. Open skies and panoramic views abound in this remote and beautiful area. Langthwaite is the largest settlement in Arkengarthdale. Its stone cottages huddle together haphazardly alongside Arkle Beck, three miles north-west of Reeth in Swaledale

To walk over the packhorse bridge and into the tiny village of Langthwaite is like stepping back in time. Stroll through the village and follow the steep single track lane up towards Booze (ironically, a village without a pub!) and soak up the scenery. In spring there are many wild flowers along this track and as you gain height the views across Arkengarthdale are simply stunning. Looking back over the village can be seen the unusual "Waterloo" church of 1817. After the French Revolution many churches of this type were built in an attempt to counteract atheism and free thinking.

Although the upper fells are scarred with the remains of 18th and 19th-century lead-mining the Dales' place names – Langthwaite, Booze, Arkle, Whaw and Eskeleth – point to that of a Norse settlement.

Meadow cranesbill *Geranium pratense*

LEYBURN

Leyburn developed quite naturally as a market town since it is situated at the junction of four main roads on the important A684 trans-Pennine route between Kendal in Cumbria and Northallerton in North Yorkshire

Although Leyburn is the main commercial, market and trading centre for lower Wensleydale, it did not receive its charter until 1684. The area is well-known for fabulous views of Wensleydale from Leyburn Shawl, a grassy terrace high above the valley to the west of the town which is easily reached from Shawl Terrace at the top of the Market Place.

The people of Leyburn certainly know how to celebrate. Each year at the beginning of May the town hosts the Dales Festival of Food and Drink. The event has developed into a very popular and exciting festival lasting three days. The Richmond Pipe Band (below) can always be relied upon to thrill and entertain at this and many

other events in the area.

The Elite Cinema (above) is a small independent venue showing a varied programme of films from art-house to Hollywood. There is a comfortable bar, and occasionally live theatre and music events are staged. The auditorium seats 173 people.

Leyburn is linked to its near neighbour Middleham by a suspension bridge. One of the first to be constructed, it was built in 1829 to ford the River Ure which runs through the whole of Wensleydale before meandering towards the Vale of York.

LINTON

A characterful village of stone cottages seven miles north of Skipton built in clusters around the village green. The green slopes eastwards towards the grassy banks of Linton Beck

There are many elegant stone houses in this picturesque village. It was voted the "prettiest village in the North" in 1949 and it appears that very little has changed since then. Linton is situated one mile south of Grassington just off the B6160; a very unusual building by the green, the Fontaine Hospital, was built in 1721 as almshouses for six poor men or women.

Linton Beck flows through the middle of the village and is crossed by a packhorse bridge, a modern road bridge, a clapper bridge, stepping stones and fords. Just one mile from the village waterfalls, a weir, riverside paths and the delightful St Michael's Church all wait to be discovered along the river Wharfe.

There is always a warm welcome at the Fontaine Inn, seen here by the large, irregular village green.

MALHAM

Malham and Malhamdale is immensely popular with visitors, surrounded as it is by some of this country's most beautiful and spectacular landscape features. The village lies just five miles west of Settle and two and a half miles south of Malham Tarn on the Pennine Way

Malham Cove, Gordale Scar, Janet's Foss Waterfall (below right) and Malham Tarn are all located at 1,229ft (375m) above sea level. They are all unique and impressive landscape features. Malham Cove is just three-quarters of a mile north of the village, and at 250ft (76m) high and over 300 yards (275m) long, is a magnificent vertical limestone rockface. At the base of the cove, as if by magic, Malham Beck appears then flows gently down through the village before making its way into the river Aire.

Malham Tarn is a very large lake formed by glaciation in the last ice age, with abundant birdlife, making it very popular with birdwatchers. Charles Kingsley set the opening scenes of his classic children's novel *The Water Babies* here. The nature reserve at the tarn attracts many visitors and the walks around the tarn are delightful. There is a National Trust visitor centre at Tarn House.

Two miles north of Gordale Scar can be found the remains of a Roman camp and from here Mastiles Lane leads west across the moor to the village of Kilnsey in Wharfedale. Just one mile south of Mastiles Lane lies the remote and pretty hamlet of Bordley.

MASHAM

Masham (pronounced "Massum") is a peaceful and attractive small market town situated midway between Ripon and Leyburn on the A6108

✍

This delightful town has many attractions including a generous cobbled marketplace surrounded by elegant Georgian houses and stone cottages, shops, galleries, workshops and tea rooms. Other attractions nearby include Jervaulx Abbey and Leighton Reservoirs. Masham's reputation amongst the beer-drinking fraternity rests with the famous Black Sheep Brewery, which was established in the early nineties. Its first brews were sampled in 1992. There is a visitor centre at the brewery and tours are very popular indeed.

The Masham Steam Engine and Fair Organ rally is a spectacular event which takes place in July. On display this particular year was the most famous showman's engine, *The Iron Maiden*

MIDDLEHAM

Just two miles south from Leyburn on the A6108, Middleham is dominated by its castle,
which can be seen for miles around

Middleham Castle was built around 1170 by Robert Fitz Randolph during the reign of Henry II. The keep has 12ft (3.5m) thick walls and is one of the largest in England. Middleham is mentioned in the Domesday Book as "Medelai" and there has been a settlement here since Roman times.

The village is situated between Coverdale and Wensleydale and is a historic centre for the training of racehorses. The Middleham Trainers Association represents trainers in the town and district, in the whole of North Yorkshire and England.

In 1985 Ted Seaton was using a metal-detector near the castle when he discovered a gold pendant weighing 2.3 ounces (68g) together with a magnificent blue sapphire. The pendant dated from the 15th-century and is now known as the Middleham Jewel; when it was sold at auction it reached the amazing sum of £1.3m. The Yorkshire Museum, in York, has since raised £2.5m to acquire the now world-famous jewel, and keep it in this country.

MIDDLESMOOR

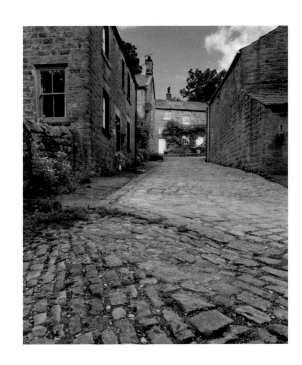

*Just seven miles north-west of Pateley Bridge at the head of Nidderdale,
Middlesmoor clings to the top of a large hill, its stone cottages and cobbled streets
huddled together to form a pretty and interesting hamlet*

St Chad's Church was restored in 1866 and its set of bells was given by Mrs Barkwith in 1868. The old church was consecrated in 1484 in the reign of Richard III, at the request of the parishioners, by Drummond, Archbishop of York. The font is Anglo Saxon which suggests that an older building was there long before the present one. The spectacular view of the vale of Nidd from the churchyard is simply breathtaking.

Middlesmoor is an ideal spot for walkers: the Nidderdale Way runs through the village and Scar House Reservoir and Brimham Rocks, with its acres of stunning rock formations, are close by.

MUKER

Situated at the head of Swaledale about one mile east of Thwaite. The Muker Silver Band, formed in 1897 to celebrate Queen Victoria's Diamond Jubilee, is famous throughout the Dales. Muker, Thwaite and Keld are dominated by Kidson Hill which is over 1,600ft high

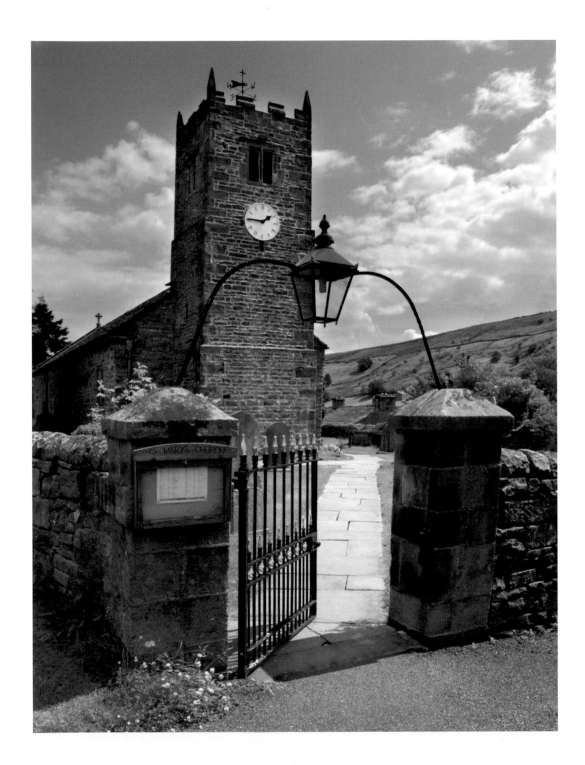

The pretty village of Muker sits proudly above Straw Beck on a long ledge. Upper Swaledale has some of the finest traditional hay meadows in the whole of the Dales and the setting is breathtaking at any time of year. Muker is a perfect place for walkers to rest on the long-distance footpath, the Pennine Way.

The village has a large number of grey stone cottages, a pub, a chapel, an institute, a craft shop, cafe, and the beautiful church of St Mary the Virgin which was one of only a few built in the reign of Elizabeth I. The colourful east window (below) was given in memory of the Rev Dr H B Wilson, Vicar of Muker (1931-1935). It depicts the scenery around the village, including the river Swale and Straw Beck, together with 23 Swaledale horned sheep – a reference to The Lord is my Shepherd (Psalm 23).

PATELEY BRIDGE

The small town of Pateley Bridge has many secrets and should not be overlooked when travelling along the B6265 in upper Nidderdale

Pateley Bridge's narrow main street is dominated by elegant dark gritstone buildings but on either side there are pretty cobbled alleyways and passages which lead to hidden and quaint courtyards with a variety of cottages, galleries and craft shops. Over the centuries Pateley Bridge developed as both a market town for the local hill farmers and an industrial centre for both textiles and lead-mining.

The townsfolk of Pateley Bridge take great pride in their spring and summer floral displays and these have won many awards over the years.

The main street has a wide variety of interesting properties and shops including the oldest sweetshop in England (above). This fascinating shop was established in 1827.

Open skies, drystone walls, panoramic views and narrow meandering lanes are all waiting to be discovered on the steep slopes that surround this sheltered settlement.

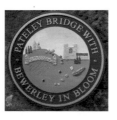

REDMIRE

Redmire lies five miles west of Leyburn on the minor road that runs along the northern side of Wensleydale

In centuries past, the village was a hive of industry and both coal and lead were mined locally; the legacy of this activity is clearly visible in the landscape to the north of the village above nearby Castle Bolton. Today's visitors will find that all traces of Redmire's industrial past have now given way to delightful cottage gardens, resplendent with flowers and vegetables. This charming, peaceful village, with its hidden nooks, crannies and riverside haunts deserves to be explored on foot. Several narrow lanes lead off the small village green which is dominated by a huge and ancient oak tree; the one which passes the smithy and the Bolton Arms leads to Castle Bolton and the road up and over the moor to Grinton in Swaledale.

Corn poppy *Papaver rhoeas*

REETH

Situated 12 miles west of Richmond on the B6270, the village was once a centre for both lead-mining and knitting, and now continues to be the market town and focal point for the local community

The village of Reeth is an immensely popular tourist centre and one can easily see why. From its elevated position the spacious, triangular village green provides stunning views of the surrounding countryside in Swaledale. In Saxon times it was a small settlement on the forest edge, but later developed and grew so that by the time of the Norman Conquest its status warranted inclusion in the Domesday Book.

August is the month for the Reeth agricultural show, a highlight of the year in Swaledale

RICHMOND

Richmond, the capital of Swaledale, is dominated by its huge and majestic castle keep, an amazing and very well-preserved piece of 12th century architecture. The town lies three and a half miles south-west of Scotch Corner on the A6108

Well before the castle was constructed in 1071 Alan Rufus started to build a fortress on the promontory beside the river Swale. The castle we see today, which is 100ft (30m) high and with walls 11ft (3.5m) thick, was built by Alan the Red of Brittany, a trusted supporter of William I, and is one of only a few Norman castles that escaped any serious siege damage. The town itself ranks among the most beautiful in England, with many elegant Georgian houses, cobbled streets, and pretty cottage gardens.

At the centre of the impressive marketplace is the 12th

century chapel of the Holy Trinity, which is now used as the regimental museum of the Green Howards. In 1788 Samuel Butler, a local actor and manager, built a small and beautiful Georgian theatre called the Theatre Royal, which is still in use and well worth a visit.

Situated in the middle of Richmond at the bottom of the marketplace

and overlooked by Millgate House, a Georgian townhouse, is a unique and beautiful south-facing walled garden. Open to the public between April and October the garden is immensely popular with visitors and should not be missed.

SETTLE

Situated just off the busy A65 Keighley to Kendal road, on the B6480 that runs northwards through Ribblesdale, the market town of Settle is a focal point for the district and very popular with visitors

Settle's market charter goes back to 1249, and together with Clapham and Ribblesdale has a close association with the famous Settle to Carlisle Railway line. The town has developed and prospered due to its location, being surrounded by mixed and arable farming together with some quite spectacular limestone scenery.

Settle is a busy market town with a quite dramatic setting. It sits snugly between the river Ribble and towering limestone crags. The market square is surrounded by 18th and 19th-century houses, shops, arcades and courtyards. The Naked Man Café, so popular with touring motorcyclists and visitors, is an enigma, as no one seems to know why the carved, almost naked, man is there. Unusually Settle does not have an ancient church, and so locals have to go to nearby Giggleswick to worship.

Scalebar Force, a beautiful cascading waterfall, is just a couple of miles from the town centre, and a short walk from the minor road that leads to Kirkby Malham.

SKIPTON

Skipton, in Airedale, lies 22 miles north-west of Leeds and is the southern gateway to the Dales. The settlement, which is now a sizeable town, dates from Anglo-Saxon times and is recorded in the Domesday Book as Sceptone which means "sheep town"

Just a few minutes walk from the hustle and bustle of Skipton's busy high street can be found this lovely stretch of the Leeds-Liverpool canal, the ideal place to stroll and contemplate, or to begin exploring the Dales in relaxing style on a canal boat (far left).

The town has a wide and colourful variety of specialist shops in the ancient courts or "folds" which lead off the high street. In the 1750s Skipton was a thriving centre for the wool trade, and it had its own livestock market. By the end of the century the canal helped bring about the establishment of the worsted cloth industry. Mills were beginning to appear around this time and the town's population grew rapidly.

Between 1650 and 1675 Lady Anne Clifford carried out extensive restoration work to Skipton castle. The medieval castle is now privately owned and is open to the public.

Holy Trinity Church has occupied its prominent position at the top of the high street since the early 1100s. Originally constructed of wood it was rebuilt in stone with the help of the monks at Bolton Priory around 1300.

Several windows in the church bear the mark of Charles Kempe (1837-1907). He is regarded as one of the giants of Victorian stained-glass craftsmanship, along with William Morris.

STAINFORTH

The small and peaceful village of Stainforth, now by-passed by the B6479, lies just two miles north of Settle. The name Stainforth is derived from the "stony ford" which once linked two separate settlements on opposite sides of the river Ribble

The narrow, high-arched 17th-century packhorse bridge (right) replaced the ford from which the village got its name and is now owned by the National Trust. The broad stone ledges provide a very popular picnic site for visitors, and early spring showers swell the rapids as they gush over Stainforth

Force. Banks of bluebells and fresh green foliage combine to make a delightful riverside setting.

Stainforth Beck flows down from Catrigg Force just one mile from the village. The waterfall is easily reached along a stony track to the east and ancient stepping stones across the beck provide relatively easy access from the centre of the village.

St Peter's Church is situated in Great Stainforth, or Stainforth-under-Bargh as it used to be known (literally "the stony ford under the hill") on the east bank of the river. Prior to the middle of the 19th century Stainforth had no church of its own, belonging to the neighbouring parish of Giggleswick. Villagers had to travel there to St Alkelda's church to worship, baptise their children, marry and bury their dead.

STARBOTTON

Starbotton, just two miles north of Kettlewell in Wharfedale, was rebuilt during the latter part of the 17th century. Its close proximity to the river Wharfe meant it was almost completely swept away during the great flood of 1686

Starbotton lies deep within the national park This photograph, left, was taken from the stony track that climbs up and out of the east side of the village, offering the serious walker an alternative route up to the summit of Buckden Pike, which at 2,302ft (701m) easily qualifies as a mountain.

The settlement of Starbotton is first mentioned in the Domesday Book. Many of its cottages and barns date from the 17th century, when they were rebuilt.

The characterful grey stone cottages in this photograph cluster snugly around the Fox and Hounds Inn which is very popular with visitors after walking along the riverside or exploring the nearby fells. Not too far away along a rough road at the back of the village are the remains of a lead smelting mill.

THWAITE

Thwaite is a delightful village situated between Keld and Muker at the western end of Swaledale on the B6270. The 52-mile long, four-day walk, the Herriot Way, passes through Thwaite

✠

Thwaite is a great centre for walkers, situated as it is on the Pennine Way and just two miles from the route of the Coast to Coast walk. It's a useful stopping-off point, going either north around Kisdon Hill or west to the summit of Great Shunner Fell, and then south to Hardraw and Hawes. The welcoming Kearton Country Hotel is very popular with visitors and is named after the

famous wildlife photographers Richard and Cherry Kearton who were born in the village.

Thwaite lies at the foot of the Buttertubs Pass, a spectacular high level moorland minor road that links Swaledale to Hawes in Wensleydale. Cliff Beck meanders through the village and later joins the river Swale near Muker.

Drystone walls, out barns, small fields and hay meadows resplendent with wildflowers – buttercups and cranesbills in late June – give Swaledale its distinct character. The northern Dales offer visitors exceptional walking country, unspoilt villages and heather-clad moorland with red grouse, lapwing and curlew.

WEST BURTON

The pretty, unspoiled village of West Burton is situated one mile south of Aysgarth on the B6160 at the northern end of Bishopdale. The large village green is surrounded by traditional Dales' stone cottages; the small road that runs through the village is unusually peaceful as it comes to a halt alongside Walden Beck

The village has two main attractions for visitors: the glorious West Burton Falls (far left), a popular location for artists and photographers, is situated to the east of the village and is easily reached on foot, while the annual May Fair, on the village green, has something for everyone and is guaranteed to draw the crowds. West Burton schoolchildren can be seen dancing around the maypole (above), while other attractions include a falconry display, a quoits knockout competition, egg-throwing and morris dancing.

The broad sweep of Wensleydale (left) has picturesque views on all sides – with or without the sheep!

WEST TANFIELD

The village of West Tanfield sits proudly beside the river Ure on the western edge of the Yorkshire Dales, just six miles north of Ripon on the A6108

Crossing the impressive stone bridge over the river, one cannot fail to be moved by the glorious aspect the village has beside the dark meandering waters of the river Ure and the surrounding countryside. The skyline of the village is dominated by both the Marmion Tower and St Nicholas's Church. The medieval parish church stands opposite the Marmion Tower, a 15th-century gatehouse noted for its great arch and oriel window. John Marmion was a knight who died while fighting in Spain under his overlord John of Gaunt, Earl of Richmond. Lady Elizabeth Marmion (neé St Quintin) may have lived in the Marmion Tower after the death of her husband, using it as a "Lady Castle" or Dower House.

The tomb (below) commemorating Sir John and Lady Elizabeth Marmion is made from Derbyshire alabaster. Sir John is wearing plate armour typical of the 14th century, and his wife's head rests upon cushions supported by angels.

Tomb commemorating Sir John Marmion who died in 1387 and Lady Elizabeth Marmion who died in 1400

WEST WITTON

Just four miles west of Leyburn on the A684, West Witton sits comfortably in the lee of Penhill which dominates the skyline in this part of Wensleydale

Wensleydale is the largest of all the Dales, a broad sweeping fertile valley in its lower reaches, which gradually closes in as you travel up the dale. At the head of the dale in the area around Hawes the landscape is more dramatic with steeper slopes leading to high windswept fells and remote winding mountain pass roads.

The photograph (right) over the gate was taken from the minor road that climbs steeply out of the village to the south and up past Penhill Farm to Melmerby. The field just beyond the gate, which belongs to Penhill Farm, is called "Bella Field". In centuries past, the whole of this part of Wensleydale was forested.

The parish church of St Bartholomew was originally Saxon, and possibly built in the sixth century. When the church was restored in 1875 the remains of a Saxon cross were found in the chancel walls. Interestingly, before 1752, the dead from West Witton were taken to Wensley for burial because the shallow depth of soil in the churchyard meant that graves could not be dug. Later, soil was brought in to alleviate the problem.

YOCKENTHWAITE

Yockenthwaite, although barely a village, is a delightfully situated small settlement in Langstrothdale about two and a half miles north-west of Buckden

The upper valley of the Wharfe above Buckden is known as Langstrothdale. In Norman times Langstrothdale Chase was a hunting preserve for game and deer, with its own forest laws, courts, punishments and privileges.

The tiny picturesque hamlet of Yockenthwaite, nestling on the hillside beside the infant river Wharfe (seen here on the right) is now merely a scattering of stone barns and traditional Dales' houses. It is, though, an ancient settlement with a Norse-Celtic name which means Egon's Clearing. A short distance upstream can be found one of only a few Bronze Age stone circles in the Dales. It has 20 stones and is approximately 25ft (7.6m) in diameter.

During the 1950s, when the Yorkshire Dales National Park was formed, many postal deliveries were still on foot. Let us hope that Yockenthwaite was an exception!

Littondale and Wharfedale from Hill Castles Scar.
This photograph was taken just a few metres from The Dales Way long-distance footpath, between
Kettlewell and Grassington, just north-east of the delightful village of Conistone in Wharfedale.
The view towards Hawkswick Moor and Middlesmoor Pasture is quite breathtaking, especially when
weather systems are racing across the dales, creating atmospheric and dramatic skies.